Copyright 2005, Gooseberry Patch
First Printing, May, 2005

All rights reserved. The patterns in this publication are the sole property of **Gooseberry Patch** and are provided for the purchaser's personal use only. Reproduction, use or distribution of the patterns for commercial purposes, without prior written consent of **Gooseberry Patch** is strictly prohibited. No other part of this book may be reproduced or utilized in any form or by any means, electronic or mechanical, including photocopying and recording, or by any information storage and retrieval system, without permission in writing from the publisher.

Need to peel tomatoes, peaches or pears in a hurry?
Simply scald them in hot water, then submerge them in
cold water...the skin will peel right off.

BLT Dip

Makes 2-1/2 cups

1 lb. bacon, crisply cooked
   and crumbled
1 c. mayonnaise

1 c. sour cream
2 tomatoes, chopped
toast rounds or snack crackers

Blend together bacon, mayonnaise and sour cream in a medium bowl. Add tomatoes just before serving. Serve with toast rounds or crackers.

Add a splash of color to sparkling cider and lemonade! Freeze grape or cranberry juice in ice cube trays and add a few cubes to each glass...so pretty!

Garden Veggie Spread

Makes 1-1/2 cups

8-oz. pkg. cream cheese, softened
1/2 c. cucumber, chopped
1 carrot, peeled and shredded
1 green onion, chopped
1 t. lemon juice
1/4 t. dill weed
assorted vegetables for dipping

Combine cream cheese, cucumber, carrot, onion, lemon juice and dill weed in a medium bowl; blend well. Chill before serving. Serve with fresh vegetables.

Make your own crunchy pita chips for dipping. Cut pita bread rounds into triangles, brush lightly with olive oil and sprinkle with garlic salt or herbs. Bake at 350 degrees for a few minutes until crisp. Yummy!

Baked Parmesan Dip

Makes 10 servings

2 8-oz. pkgs. cream cheese, softened
1/2 c. mayonnaise
2 c. grated Parmesan cheese
2/3 c. onion, diced
corn chips

Mix ingredients except corn chips together; spread in an ungreased 13"x9" baking pan. Bake at 400 degrees for 20 minutes, or until bubbly and golden. Serve with corn chips.

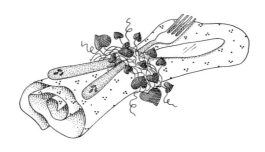

Need a variety of chopped veggies when preparing a salad or main dish? Simply stop at your grocer's salad bar for a wonderful variety of ready-to-use veggies...buy just what you need and save yourself a lot of slicing and dicing!

Super Nachos

Makes 4 to 6 servings

2 10-inch flour tortillas
3/4 c. salsa
4-oz. can diced green chiles, drained
1/2 c. sliced black olives
1 c. shredded Monterey Jack cheese

Place tortillas on an ungreased baking sheet; spread tortillas with salsa. Sprinkle chiles and olives over the salsa; top with cheese. Bake at 425 degrees for 10 minutes, or until tortillas are crisp and cheese is melted. Use a pizza cutter to slice each into 8 wedges.

A happy life is made of little things.
-Carol Holmes

Caramel Apple Dip

Makes 2 cups

8-oz. pkg. cream cheese, softened
1 c. brown sugar, packed
1 t. vanilla extract
apple wedges

Blend together cream cheese, sugar and vanilla; cover and refrigerate overnight. Serve cold, with apple wedges for dipping.

Mix up the the ingredients for this quick & easy salad in a plastic zipping bag and it'll be done in half the time. Just blend by shaking and spoon out individual servings.

Crunchy Corn Chip Salad *Makes 6 servings*

11-oz. can sweet corn & diced peppers, drained
1/3 c. green pepper, minced
1/4 c. green onion, chopped
10-oz. pkg. corn chips
8-oz. bottle ranch salad dressing

Combine corn, green pepper and green onion in a large serving bowl; refrigerate. At serving time, add corn chips and enough ranch dressing to moisten. Serve immediately.

Rub the inside of salad bowls with a halved clove of garlic...it'll add a hint of flavor to any salad.

Tomato-Feta Salad

Makes 8 to 10 servings

2 pts. cherry tomatoes, halved
1 sweet onion, chopped
4-oz. pkg. crumbled feta cheese
2/3 c. oil
1/3 c. red wine vinegar
Optional: fresh oregano, basil or chives, chopped

Gently combine tomatoes, onion and cheese in a serving bowl; set aside. Whisk together oil, vinegar and herbs, if using; pour over tomato mixture. Toss to coat; cover and refrigerate before serving.

Nestle 2 sizes of enamelware bowls together. Fill the bottom one with crushed ice and add a crispy salad to the top bowl...keeps salads cool in hot weather!

Best-Ever Broccoli Salad *Makes 6 to 8 servings*

1/2 c. mayonnaise
1/4 c. sugar
2 T. vinegar
1 head broccoli, chopped
1 sweet onion, diced
1 c. shredded Cheddar cheese
6 to 8 slices bacon, crisply
　cooked and crumbled

Whisk mayonnaise, sugar and vinegar together; set aside. Combine broccoli, onion, cheese and bacon in a serving bowl. Pour mayonnaise mixture over the top, tossing gently. Serve immediately.

Short on time? Pick up some pre-shredded coleslaw mix in the produce aisle for this recipe...what a time-saver!

Country Coleslaw

Makes 6 servings

3 c. shredded cabbage
1 c. carrot, peeled and shredded
1/2 c. whipping cream
3 T. cider vinegar
salt and pepper to taste

In a large bowl, combine cabbage and carrot. In a separate small bowl, whip the cream and vinegar slowly. Add salt and pepper; pour over cabbage mixture and toss to coat. Chill before serving.

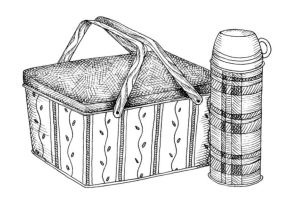

Packing a salad for a picnic or in lunch boxes? Freeze a few juice boxes and they'll keep the whole lunch cool!

Redskin Potato Salad

Makes 6 to 8 servings

8 to 10 redskin potatoes, cooked and cubed
2 to 3 green onions, chopped
1 to 2 c. ranch salad dressing
salt and pepper to taste

Combine potatoes and onions in a large bowl. Stir in ranch dressing; season with salt and pepper. Serve chilled.

Keep a spray mister full of lime or lemon juice in the fridge. So handy for spritzing sliced pears, apples or peaches...adds extra zing and prevents browning too!

Waldorf Salad *Makes 4 servings*

1 c. apples, cored and diced
1 c. celery, diced
1/2 c. chopped walnuts

3/4 c. mayonnaise
salt to taste

Gently fold ingredients together in a serving bowl. Cover and chill until serving time.

Yogurt is a great healthy substitute for sour cream. Try plain yogurt in savory main dishes and vanilla or fruit-flavored yogurt in sweet dishes.

5-Cup Ambrosia Salad

Makes 6 servings

1 c. pineapple tidbits, drained
1 c. mandarin oranges, drained
1 c. mini marshmallows
1 c. flaked coconut
1 c. sour cream

Gently stir ingredients together in a serving bowl. Cover and chill until serving time.

Line the inside of a cabinet door with self-stick cork tiles to make an oh-so-handy bulletin board. It'll be a great place to tack quick recipes, take-out menus, emergency numbers and more!

Parmesan-Garlic Biscuits *Makes 8 servings*

3 T. butter, melted
1/4 t. celery seed
2 cloves garlic, minced

12-oz. tube refrigerated biscuits
2 T. grated Parmesan cheese

Coat the bottom of a 9" pie plate with butter; add celery seed and garlic. Cut each biscuit into quarters; arrange on top of butter mixture. Sprinkle with Parmesan cheese. Bake at 425 degrees for 12 to 15 minutes. Invert onto a serving plate to serve.

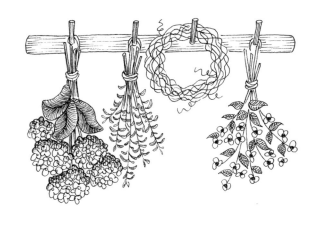

Add freshly snipped herbs like basil, dill or thyme
to biscuit dough for delicious variety.

Onion Dinner Rolls

Makes 6 servings

1/2 c. butter, melted
1-1/2 t. dried parsley
1/2 t. dill weed
1 T. dried, minced onion

2 T. grated Parmesan cheese
10-oz. tube refrigerated
   buttermilk biscuits

Place melted butter in a bowl; stir in herbs, onion and Parmesan cheese. Cut each biscuit into quarters; dip into butter mixture, coating all sides. Arrange biscuits in a greased 9"x9" baking pan; bake at 425 degrees for 15 minutes.

Glass or dark baking pans will retain more heat than shiny ones. Be sure to reduce the oven temperature by 25 degrees when using them.

Melt-Away Biscuits

Makes 12 to 14 servings

1 c. butter, melted
1 c. sour cream

2 c. self-rising flour

Blend butter and sour cream together; mix in flour. Fill lightly greased muffin cups 2/3 full with batter. Bake at 350 degrees for 30 minutes.

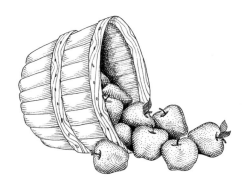

To give your warm-from-the-oven bread a sweet, shiny glaze, brush with honey...it also absorbs moisture and bread will stay fresh longer.

Applesauce Spice Muffins

Makes 12 servings

2 c. biscuit baking mix
1/2 c. milk
2 T. sugar
1/4 c. applesauce

2 T. brown sugar, packed
1/2 t. cinnamon
1/2 t. nutmeg

Combine all ingredients in a medium bowl; stir together for one minute with a wooden spoon. Fill greased muffin cups 2/3 full. Bake at 350 degrees for 15 minutes.

The kids will love eating "ears" of cornbread... just spoon the batter into vintage corn-shaped pans!

Maple Cornbread

Makes 9 to 12 servings

1 c. plus 2 T. cornmeal
1 c. plus 2 T. whole-wheat flour
1 T. baking powder
1/2 t. salt

1 egg, beaten
1/2 c. maple syrup
3/4 c. milk
3 T. shortening, melted

In a large bowl, mix cornmeal, flour, baking powder and salt. Add remaining ingredients; stir until well blended but do not beat. Pour into a greased 9"x9" baking pan or 12 greased muffin cups. Bake at 400 degrees for 20 minutes.

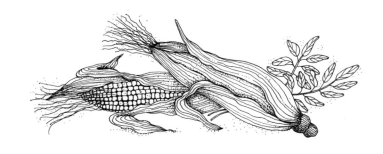

Toting a casserole to a get-together? Wrap it up in a cheery bandanna and tie the knot at the top...an ideal spot to slip in a serving spoon!

Cornbread Corn Casserole   *Makes 15 to 18 servings*

8-1/2 oz. pkg. corn muffin mix
2 15-oz. cans creamed corn
1 egg, beaten
1/3 c. butter, melted
3/4 c. sour cream

Combine ingredients; pour into a greased 13"x9" baking pan. Bake at 375 degrees for 35 to 45 minutes.

A big chalkboard in the kitchen is a handy spot to keep a running grocery list.

Smoky Green Beans

Makes 4 servings

4 slices hickory-smoked bacon, diced
1 sweet onion, diced
24-oz. can green beans
8-oz. can tomato sauce

In a large skillet over medium heat, sauté bacon and onion together for 15 minutes, stirring often. Add beans and their liquid; stir in tomato sauce. Reduce heat, cover and simmer for one hour.

Cutting up veggies for dinner? Go ahead and cut up some extra for lunch the next day. Save time in the morning and clean up once instead of twice!

French-Fried Cauliflower   *Makes 6 to 8 servings*

1 head cauliflower, cut into flowerets
3 eggs, beaten
1 sleeve round buttery crackers, crushed
oil for deep frying

Dip cauliflower into beaten eggs; coat with cracker crumbs. Deep fry until golden in a heavy skillet with 1/2 inch oil. Place on paper towels to drain.

Cheese always makes dinner more tasty! Split
brown & serve dinner rolls partly in half and sprinkle Cheddar
or Swiss cheese, chopped green onion or parsley inside. Bake
until golden and enjoy.

Herbed Corn Bake *Makes 4 servings*

1/4 c. butter
1/2 c. cream cheese, softened
1/4 t. onion salt
1 T. fresh chives, chopped
10-oz. pkg. frozen corn, thawed

Melt butter in a heavy saucepan. Add cream cheese, onion salt and chives, stirring until cheese melts. Add corn; mix well. Pour into an ungreased 1-1/2 quart casserole dish. Cover and bake at 325 degrees until bubbly, about 45 minutes.

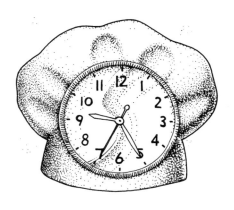

Save time by putting the food processor to work
chopping and dicing veggies...so easy!

Baked Zucchini Gratin

Makes 8 servings

1 onion, sliced
2 lbs. zucchini, sliced
1/2 c. butter, melted and divided
2 c. shredded mozzarella cheese
1/2 c. bread crumbs
1/4 c. grated Parmesan cheese

Layer onion and zucchini in a lightly greased 2-quart baking dish. Drizzle with 1/4 cup butter; sprinkle with mozzarella cheese. In a separate bowl, combine remaining butter, bread crumbs and Parmesan cheese. Sprinkle crumb mixture evenly over the top. Bake, uncovered, at 350 degrees for 35 to 40 minutes, or until zucchini is tender.

Stuffed burgers turn ordinary into an extraordinary dinner! Form a thin patty and top with a sprinkle of cheese, roasted garlic, bacon crumbles, salsa or fresh herbs. Place another thin patty on top and carefully seal the edges. Grill as usual and enjoy!

Cheesy Hashbrowns

Makes 8 to 10 servings

30-oz. pkg. frozen shredded
    hashbrowns, thawed
2 c. sour cream
2 10-3/4 oz. cans cream of
    mushroom soup
1 onion, chopped
3 c. shredded Cheddar cheese,
    divided

Combine hashbrowns, sour cream, soup, onion and 2 cups cheese; mix well. Spread in a lightly greased 13"x9" baking pan; sprinkle with remaining cheese. Bake at 350 degrees for one hour.

When a recipe calls for pasta, there's so many shapes to choose from, why not experiment? Try using corkscrew, shell, bow tie and tricolor pasta just for fun!

15-Minute Parmesan Pasta

Makes 4 servings

8-oz. pkg. pasta, cooked
1 clove garlic, minced
1/4 c. olive oil
3/4 c. grated Parmesan cheese

Keep pasta warm in a large serving bowl. Sauté garlic in oil until golden and tender; pour over pasta. Add cheese; toss gently to coat. Serve immediately.

The kitchen is the heart of the home,
and the mother is queen of the kitchen.
-Owen Meredith

Scalloped Pineapple

Makes 12 servings

1/2 c. butter, sliced
4 c. soft bread crumbs
2 c. sugar
3 eggs, beaten
1/2 c. evaporated milk
16-oz. can crushed pineapple
Garnish: cinnamon

Combine all ingredients except cinnamon in a medium bowl. Mix well and pour into an ungreased 13"x9" baking dish. Bake, uncovered, at 350 degrees for 45 to 55 minutes. Sprinkle with cinnamon at serving time.

Before marinating chicken, pour some marinade into a plastic squeeze bottle for easy basting...how clever!

Sweet & Spicy Chicken

Makes 6 servings

6 boneless, skinless chicken breasts
1/2 c. orange juice
1/4 c. honey
1-oz. pkg. Italian salad dressing mix

Place chicken in a glass dish; set aside. Mix remaining ingredients and pour over chicken. Marinate for one hour, turning to coat both sides; discard marinade. Grill or broil chicken until juices run clear when pierced with a fork.

The next time mashed potatoes are on the dinner menu, whip in a teaspoon or so of baking powder and they'll be extra light and fluffy...don't forget the butter!

Savory Chicken Casserole

Makes 6 servings

10-3/4 oz. can cream of mushroom soup
10-3/4 oz. can cream of celery soup
1 c. milk
1 c. instant rice, uncooked
2 to 3 lbs. chicken
1-1/2 oz. pkg. onion soup mix
1 t. garlic, minced
1 t. onion salt

Mix soups, milk and rice together; spread in a greased 13"x9" baking pan. Arrange chicken over top; sprinkle with soup mix, garlic and onion salt. Bake at 350 degrees for 40 to 45 minutes, until juices run clear when chicken is pierced.

Instead of serving traditional biscuits or dinner rolls with this dish, bake up some sweet and tangy cranberry muffins! Just stir frozen cranberries into cornbread muffin mix and bake as usual.

Swiss Chicken & Stuffing

Makes 4 to 6 servings

4 to 6 boneless, skinless chicken breasts
4 to 6 slices Swiss cheese
10-3/4 oz. can cream of chicken soup
1/4 c. water
2 c. herb-flavored stuffing mix
1/3 c. butter, melted

Arrange chicken in a 2-quart casserole dish. Place one slice of cheese on top of each piece of chicken. Combine soup and water; spoon evenly over chicken. Sprinkle stuffing mix over the top; drizzle with melted butter. Bake, uncovered, at 350 degrees for 35 minutes, until chicken juices run clear when pierced.

Fresh out of bread crumbs for this crunchy coating? Use herb-flavored stuffing mix in their place and it'll be just as yummy!

Parmesan Baked Chicken   *Makes 4 servings*

1/2 c. mayonnaise-type salad dressing
1/3 c. grated Parmesan cheese
3/4 t. garlic powder
4 boneless, skinless chicken breasts
3/4 c. Italian-flavored dry bread crumbs

Combine salad dressing, Parmesan cheese and garlic powder in a mixing bowl. Coat chicken with mixture; cover each with bread crumbs. Arrange chicken in an ungreased baking dish. Bake at 425 degrees for 15 to 20 minutes, or until lightly golden and juices run clear when chicken is pierced.

Keep a pair of scissors in the kitchen to make quick work of dicing tomatoes, shredding lettuce, chopping celery and even cutting up chicken for casseroles!

Creamy Chicken Spaghetti   *Makes 8 servings*

- 2 10-3/4 oz. cans cream of chicken soup
- 10-3/4 oz. can cream of mushroom soup
- 8-oz. pkg. pasteurized process cheese spread, cubed
- 2 lbs. chicken breasts, cooked and shredded
- 2 14-1/2 oz. cans diced tomatoes
- 4-oz. can sliced mushrooms, drained
- 16-oz. pkg. spaghetti, cooked

Combine soups and cheese spread in a saucepan. Heat over medium heat until cheese is melted. Gently stir in remaining ingredients and heat through.

Dip your hands into cold water before shaping meatballs...they won't stick to your hands.

BBQ Turkey Meatballs *Makes 4 servings*

1 lb. ground turkey
1 onion, minced
1 egg, beaten
1/2 c. bread crumbs
1 T. milk
1 t. salt

1 c. catsup
1 clove garlic, minced
1/2 c. brown sugar, packed
1/4 c. lemon juice
1 T. Worcestershire sauce
salt and pepper to taste

Combine first 6 ingredients; mix well. Form into 12 balls; set aside. Add remaining ingredients to a Dutch oven; bring to a boil over medium heat. Add meatballs; cover and simmer until browned, about 20 to 25 minutes.

Spice up south-of-the-border casseroles...instead of Cheddar cheese, try Mexican-blend or Pepper Jack cheese. Zesty!

Crunchy Corn Chip Chicken

Makes 6 servings

6 boneless, skinless chicken breasts
10-3/4 oz. can cream of chicken soup
2 c. shredded Cheddar cheese, divided
1-1/4 oz. pkg. taco seasoning mix
2 c. barbecue corn chips, crushed

Arrange chicken in an ungreased 13"x9" baking pan; set aside. Combine soup, one cup cheese and taco seasoning; spread over chicken. Bake at 450 degrees for 45 minutes; sprinkle with crushed chips and remaining cheese. Return to oven and bake until cheese melts, about 5 minutes.

If your favorite casserole drips in the oven, place a sheet of aluminum foil under the pan to catch drippings...clean-up is a snap!

Cheeseburger Bake *Makes 4 servings*

8-oz. tube refrigerated crescent rolls
1 lb. ground beef
1-1/4 oz. pkg. taco seasoning mix
15-oz. can tomato sauce
2 c. shredded Cheddar cheese

Unroll crescent roll dough; press into a greased 9" round baking pan, pinching seams closed. Bake at 350 degrees for 10 minutes; set aside. Brown ground beef in a skillet over medium heat; drain. Add taco seasoning and tomato sauce to skillet; heat through, about 7 minutes. Pour into crust; sprinkle cheese on top. Bake for 10 to 15 minutes at 350 degrees. Let stand for 5 minutes before serving.

Making your favorite casserole? Make an extra to freeze...
enjoy the next time you need a quick dinner!

Salisbury Steak

Makes 6 servings

1-1/2 lbs. ground beef
1/4 c. round buttery crackers, crushed
1 egg, beaten
1 onion, chopped
10-3/4 oz. can cream of mushroom soup
1 T. mustard
1 T. horseradish sauce
1 t. Worcestershire sauce
1/2 c. water
2 T. dried parsley

Combine ground beef, crackers, egg and onion; set aside. Mix soup, mustard and sauces together in a medium bowl; add 1/4 cup to meat mixture. Form meat into 6 patties; brown on both sides in a skillet and drain. Stir water and parsley into remaining soup mixture; pour over patties. Simmer for 20 minutes.

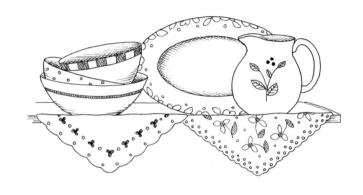

To thicken gravy, add a few instant potato flakes. It will be hearty and extra yummy.

Stroganoff Skillet

Makes 4 to 6 servings

1 lb. ground beef
1 onion, chopped
10-3/4 oz. can cream of
 mushroom soup
1 c. sour cream
1 c. beef broth
1/2 c. water
3 c. wide egg noodles, uncooked

Brown ground beef and onion in a large skillet over medium heat; drain. Gradually blend in remaining ingredients. Bring to a boil; reduce heat, cover and simmer for 10 minutes, or until noodles are tender.

Look for festive sombreros at party supply stores...line with brightly colored cloth napkins and serve up tortilla chips in style!

Tex-Mex Chili

Makes 4 servings

1 lb. ground beef, browned and drained
15-oz. can hot chili beans
15-1/2 oz. can kidney beans
12-oz. jar salsa
1-1/4 oz. pkg. chili seasoning mix
1/2 to 1 c. water

Combine all ingredients in a large stockpot. Bring to a boil over medium heat; reduce heat and simmer for 10 to 15 minutes.

Spray plastic storage containers with non-stick vegetable spray before pouring in tomato-based sauces...no stains!

Cheesy Macaroni & Beef

Makes 4 to 6 servings

2 7-1/4 oz. pkgs. macaroni & cheese
1 to 1-1/2 lbs. ground beef
14-oz. can stewed tomatoes, drained
26-oz. jar spaghetti sauce
8-oz. pkg. shredded mozzarella cheese

Prepare macaroni & cheese according to package directions; set aside. Brown ground beef in a large skillet; drain, then stir in tomatoes and spaghetti sauce. Combine with macaroni & cheese; spoon into an ungreased 13"x9" baking dish. Sprinkle with cheese. Bake, uncovered, at 350 degrees for 20 minutes.

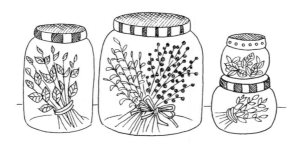

When freezing ground beef, why not brown it first? Add any seasonings, drain and cool before placing recipe-size portions into freezer bags...they'll be ready for all those quick & easy meals!

Simple Sloppy Joes   *Makes 6 to 8 servings*

1 lb. ground beef
1 onion, chopped
1 c. catsup
2 T. Worcestershire sauce
1/4 c. water
1/4 t. salt
1/4 t. pepper
6 to 8 sandwich buns

Brown beef with onion; drain. Stir in catsup, Worcestershire sauce, water, salt and pepper; simmer for 20 minutes, stirring frequently. Spoon onto buns.

Put dinner on the to-do list and resist the urge to answer phone messages or read the mail. Focusing on the task at hand will help make a meal faster and easier too!

Wagon Wheel Skillet   *Makes 5 to 6 servings*

1 T. dried, minced onion
1/2 c. milk
1-1/2 lbs. ground beef
1 egg, beaten
1/2 c. quick-cooking oats, uncooked
2 t. salt
1/4 t. pepper
browning and seasoning sauce to taste
1 c. spaghetti sauce with mushrooms
1 c. kidney beans

Soak onion in milk for 5 minutes; mix in beef, egg, oats, salt and pepper. Mound in a large skillet; score into 5 to 6 wedges. Brush top lightly with browning sauce; set aside. Combine spaghetti sauce and kidney beans; pour over meat. Simmer, uncovered, until done, about 25 to 30 minutes.

Freeze homemade mashed potatoes in individual muffin cups. Once they're frozen, pop them out, store in plastic freezer bags and just microwave as needed.

Mini Meatloaves

Makes 6 servings

1 lb. ground beef
1 onion, chopped
2 slices bread, cubed
1 egg
10-3/4 oz. can vegetable soup

Combine all ingredients in a large bowl. Shape into 12 equal portions; place in ungreased muffin cups. Bake at 350 degrees for 15 to 20 minutes.

An easy way to beef up any recipe...crumble leftover meatloaf or cut roast beef into bite-size pieces, season to taste and toss into casseroles, soups and sauces.

Noodle Casserole

Makes 4 to 6 servings

8-oz. pkg. fine egg noodles, cooked
1 T. margarine
1 c. sour cream
1 c. cottage cheese
1 lb. ground beef, browned and drained
15-oz. can tomato sauce
1/2 c. green onion, chopped
1 t. salt
1/4 t. garlic salt
1/8 t. pepper
1 c. shredded Cheddar cheese

Combine all ingredients except Cheddar cheese; spread in a 2-quart casserole dish. Sprinkle Cheddar cheese on top. Bake at 350 degrees until bubbly, about 30 minutes.

No cooked, cubed ham on hand? Chop up some slices of cooked deli ham to use instead. Deli turkey, chicken and even roast beef can all be used in place of cooked meats in recipes...what a timesaver!

Ham & Green Bean Supper *Makes 6 to 8 servings*

2 to 3 lbs. cooked ham, cubed
6 potatoes, peeled, cooked
  and cubed
2 14-1/2 oz. cans green beans,
  drained
1/2 c. onion, chopped
2 10-3/4 oz. cans cream
  of chicken soup
1 t. garlic powder
1/2 c. bread crumbs

Stir together all ingredients except for bread crumbs; spread in a lightly greased 13"x9" baking pan. Sprinkle with crumbs; bake at 350 degrees for 45 minutes.

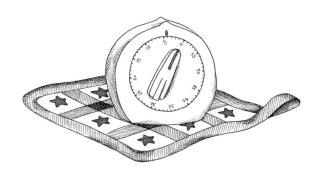

Freezing cooked rice makes for quick-fix meals later. Use it for stir-fry dishes, to make soups thick & hearty or mix in fresh vegetables for an easy side dish... just freeze servings flat in plastic zipping bags.

Saucy Pork Chops

Makes 4 to 6 servings

4 to 6 pork chops
2 10-3/4 oz. cans cream of
   chicken soup
1/2 c. catsup
2 T. Worcestershire sauce
2-1/2 c. prepared rice

Arrange pork chops in an ungreased 13"x9" baking pan; set aside. Mix soup, catsup and Worcestershire sauce together; pour over chops. Cover and bake for one hour at 350 degrees. Serve each pork chop on a portion of prepared rice; spoon remaining sauce over top.

Sharing a casserole? Be sure to tie on a tag with the recipe. Clever tags can be made from almost anything...mailing or gift tags, decorative notecards, ribbons and colorful labels!

Ham & Noodle Skillet

Makes 4 servings

4-oz. can sliced mushrooms
2 c. cooked ham, cubed
1/4 c. onion, chopped
2 T. margarine
1/8 t. pepper
1/8 t. paprika
1 t. Worcestershire sauce
1 c. water
1-1/2 c. medium egg noodles, uncooked
1 c. sour cream

Drain mushrooms; reserve 1/4 cup liquid and set aside. Sauté ham and onion in margarine in a skillet; stir in pepper, paprika and Worcestershire sauce. Add water, reserved mushroom liquid and noodles; bring to a boil. Reduce heat; simmer, covered, for 15 minutes or until noodles are tender. Stir in mushrooms; heat an additional 5 minutes. Add sour cream; heat through without boiling.

Place onions in the freezer for 5 minutes before slicing them...no more tears!

Quick Tuna Casserole *Makes 4 servings*

1-1/2 c. elbow macaroni, cooked
10-3/4 oz. can cream of mushroom soup
6-oz. can tuna, drained
5-oz. can evaporated milk
1/2 c. shredded Cheddar cheese
1/3 c. onion, chopped
3 c. potato chips, crushed

Combine all ingredients except potato chips in an ungreased 9"x9" baking dish. Top with chips. Bake, uncovered, at 425 degrees for 15 minutes, until hot and bubbly.

Whip up a tasty sauce for salmon or crab cakes...whisk together 1/2 cup sour cream, 1-1/2 tablespoons Dijon mustard, a tablespoon of lemon juice and 2 teaspoons of dill weed. Chill...so simple, so good!

Summertime Salmon Cakes *Makes 2 to 4 servings*

2 6-oz. cans salmon, drained
2 eggs, beaten
10 saltine crackers, crushed

salt and pepper to taste
olive oil

Mix together salmon, eggs and crackers; add salt and pepper to taste. Form into patties. Heat oil in a skillet; sauté patties on both sides until golden.

Baking soda can bring out the natural sweetness of tomato sauce by reducing the acid. Add about 1/4 teaspoon per quart of sauce as it simmers.

No-Fuss Tomato Sauce

Makes 3-1/2 cups

28-oz. can crushed tomatoes
2 T. olive oil
2 cloves garlic, minced
salt and pepper to taste
cooked pasta

Combine tomatoes, oil and garlic in a heavy saucepan. Simmer until thickened, about 20 minutes. Add salt and pepper to taste. Serve over hot cooked pasta.

When freezing leftover diced peppers, corn or fresh herbs,
add a little olive oil to the plastic zipping bag and shake.
The oil will help keep the food separate and fresher too.
They'll be ready to drop into sauces, salsas and salads!

Zippy Ziti & Broccoli

Makes 4 to 6 servings

8-oz. pkg. ziti pasta, uncooked
2 c. frozen broccoli cuts
1 clove garlic, minced
17-oz. jar Alfredo sauce
14-1/2 oz. can Italian-style diced tomatoes
2 c. shredded mozzarella cheese
2 T. Italian-flavored dry bread crumbs
2 t. margarine, melted

Prepare ziti according to package directions; add broccoli during last minute of cooking time. Drain; add garlic, Alfredo sauce, tomatoes and cheese, mixing well. Spoon into an ungreased 2-quart casserole dish; set aside. Toss bread crumbs with margarine; sprinkle over ziti. Bake at 350 degrees until top is golden, about 20 to 30 minutes.

Leftover chicken? Shred and toss it in this zesty casserole....serve up some Spanish rice on the side!

Easy Enchilada Casserole *Makes 6 servings*

15-oz. bag tortilla chips, divided
2 c. shredded Cheddar cheese, divided
10-3/4 oz. can cream of chicken soup
10-oz. can enchilada sauce
16-oz. can green chile sauce

Arrange a layer of chips in the bottom of a greased 13"x9" casserole dish; sprinkle one cup Cheddar cheese on top. Stir soup and sauces together in a bowl; pour half over cheese layer. Add another layer of chips; spread with remaining sauce mixture. Sprinkle with remaining cheese; bake at 400 degrees for 30 minutes.

Line your baking pan with aluminum foil...be sure to grease. After bar cookies are baked and cooled, they lift right out. And best of all, clean-up is a breeze!

Easy Butterscotch Bars

Makes 2 dozen

12-oz. pkg. butterscotch chips, melted
1 c. butter, softened
1/2 c. brown sugar, packed
1/2 c. sugar
3 eggs
1-1/2 t. vanilla extract
2 c. all-purpose flour

Combine butterscotch chips and butter; mix well. Add sugars, eggs and vanilla; gradually blend in flour. Pour into a lightly greased 13"x9" baking pan; bake at 350 degrees for 40 minutes. Let cool and cut into squares.

Need to chop nuts in a hurry? Place them in a plastic zipping bag and roll with a rolling pin...so easy!

Peanut Butter-Chocolate Bars

Makes 2 to 2-1/2 dozen

1 c. creamy peanut butter
1 c. butter, melted
1 c. graham cracker crumbs
16-oz. pkg. powdered sugar
2 c. semi-sweet chocolate chips, melted

Combine peanut butter, butter, cracker crumbs and powdered sugar in a large mixing bowl; mix well using a wooden spoon. Press into the bottom of a well-greased jelly-roll pan; pour melted chocolate evenly over top. Refrigerate for 15 minutes; score into bars but leave in pan. Return to refrigerator until firm; slice completely through scores. Keep chilled.

Before cubing angel food cake, freeze and then partially thaw it. Fewer crumbs and more to enjoy!

Angel's Delight

Makes 18 to 24 servings

5.1-oz. pkg. instant vanilla pudding mix
1 angel food cake, cut into cubes
15-1/4 oz. can sliced peaches, drained
2 8-oz. containers frozen whipped topping, thawed

Prepare pudding according to package directions; refrigerate for about 10 minutes. Line the bottom of an ungreased 13"x9" baking pan with cake cubes; spread pudding over cake. Arrange peaches over top; spread whipped topping over all. Cover and refrigerate for about one hour.

Put out the welcome mat and invite friends over for dessert...keep it simple so everyone's free to visit.

Pineapple-Cherry Cake

Makes 15 servings

20-oz. can crushed pineapple
18-1/4 oz. pkg. yellow cake
  mix, divided
15-1/2 oz. can pitted cherries,
  drained
1 c. chopped walnuts or pecans
1 c. butter, melted

Spread pineapple evenly in an ungreased 13"x9" baking pan. Sprinkle half the dry cake mix on top; spread cherries over cake mix. Sprinkle on remaining cake mix; add nuts. Drizzle with butter; bake at 350 degrees for 45 to 50 minutes.

Brewed coffee adds a rich taste to chocolate recipes...just substitute for an equal amount of water or milk in cake, cookie or brownie recipes.

Cookies & Cream Dessert *Makes 15 servings*

20-oz. pkg. chocolate sandwich cookies, crushed
1/4 c. margarine, melted
2 8-oz. pkgs. cream cheese, softened
2 8-oz. containers frozen whipped topping, thawed and divided
2 3.9-oz. pkgs. instant chocolate pudding mix

Mix cookie crumbs with margarine; press into the bottom of an ungreased 13"x9" baking pan. Combine cream cheese with one container whipped topping; spread over cookie layer. Prepare pudding according to package directions; spread on top of cream cheese mixture. Top with remaining whipped topping; refrigerate until firm.

Non-stick vegetable spray can usually be used instead of shortening to prepare baking sheets and baking dishes. One spritz and you're ready to bake!

Triple Fudge Cake

Makes 18 servings

3.4-oz. pkg. cook & serve
 chocolate pudding mix
18-1/2 oz. pkg. chocolate
 cake mix

12-oz. pkg. semi-sweet
 chocolate chips

Prepare pudding according to package directions; stir in dry cake mix. Spread in a greased 13"x9" baking pan; sprinkle with chocolate chips. Bake at 350 degrees for 35 minutes; let cool.

Make memories with those you love...spend a day baking and sharing favorite recipes.

Chocolate Chip Cookie Dough Pie *Makes 8 servings*

18-oz. tube refrigerated chocolate chip cookie dough
2 8-oz. pkgs. cream cheese, softened
2 eggs, beaten
5 1.4-oz. bars chocolate covered toffee candy, crushed

Press cookie dough into an ungreased 9" pie plate; set aside. Combine remaining ingredients in a large bowl; pour over top of dough. Bake at 325 degrees for 30 to 35 minutes. Refrigerate immediately and chill until firm.

Keep cookies moist! Place one slice of bread into a cookie jar or the storage bag and your treats will stay soft.

Speedy Peanut Butter Cookies *Makes 12 to 15*

1 c. sugar
1 c. creamy peanut butter
1 egg

Blend ingredients together; let stand for 5 minutes. Scoop dough with a small ice cream scoop; place 2 inches apart on ungreased baking sheets. Use the tines of a fork to make a criss-cross pattern on top of each cookie. Bake at 350 degrees for 10 to 12 minutes. Let cool on baking sheets for 5 minutes; remove to wire rack to finish cooling.

Lunch treats in a flash! Pack small plastic zipping bags with a few cookies each...place all the little bags into one big freezer bag. Freeze and use for lunches as needed!

BIG Chocolate Cookies *Makes 6 dozen*

2 18-1/4 oz. pkgs. chocolate cake mix
19.8-oz. pkg. brownie mix
3 eggs
3/4 c. oil
3/4 c. water

Combine all ingredients in a large bowl; mix well. Drop by tablespoonfuls 3 inches apart onto ungreased baking sheets. Bake at 325 degrees for 8 to 10 minutes.

A great way to keep brown sugar from hardening is to drop a slice of fresh apple in the bag...it absorbs extra moisture.

Quick Blueberry Crisp

Makes 4 to 6 servings

21-oz. can blueberry pie filling
1/2 c. quick-cooking oats, uncooked
1/2 c. all-purpose flour
1/4 c. brown sugar, packed
2 T. chopped walnuts
6 T. margarine

Spoon pie filling into a one-quart baking dish that has been sprayed with non-stick vegetable spray. Set aside. In a medium bowl, combine oats, flour, brown sugar and walnuts. Use a pastry blender or 2 knives to cut in margarine until mixture resembles coarse crumbs; sprinkle mixture over pie filling. Bake at 375 degrees for 45 minutes or until lightly golden and bubbly.

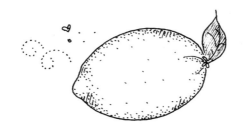

Add a pinch of cinnamon to coffee grounds before brewing...reduces bitterness and adds a touch of spice.

Lemon Pastries

Makes 16 pastries

8-oz. pkg. cream cheese, softened
1/2 c. sugar
1 T. lemon juice
2 8-oz. tubes refrigerated crescent rolls
1/2 c. powdered sugar
1 t. vanilla extract
1 to 2 T. milk

Blend cream cheese, sugar and lemon juice; set aside. Unroll crescent rolls and divide along perforations into triangles; spread with cream cheese mixture. Roll up crescent roll-style; bake on ungreased baking sheets at 350 degrees for 20 minutes. Let cool. Whisk together powdered sugar, vanilla and milk until smooth and creamy; spoon over pastries.

Roll Caramel-Marshmallow Delights in colorful jimmies or sprinkles, then insert lollipop sticks for a festive treat on-a-stick that kids will love.

Caramel-Marshmallow Delights *Makes 5 to 6 dozen*

14-oz. can sweetened condensed milk
1/2 c. butter
14-oz. pkg. caramels, unwrapped
16-oz. pkg. marshmallows
16-oz. pkg. puffed rice cereal

Combine milk, butter and caramels in a heavy saucepan over medium heat. Stir until melted and smooth; remove from heat. Using a fork, quickly dip marshmallows into mixture and then roll in rice cereal. Arrange on aluminum foil-lined baking sheets; refrigerate for 30 minutes. Remove from baking sheets; store in an airtight container in the refrigerator.

Share your favorite **Quick & Easy** recipe with friends & family!

Copy and color these fun cards to make your own personalized recipe cards!

INDEX

APPETIZERS
Baked Parmesan Dip	7
BLT Dip	3
Caramel Apple Dip	11
Garden Veggie Spread	5
Super Nachos	9

BREADS
Applesauce Spice Muffins	33
Maple Cornbread	35
Melt-Away Biscuits	31
Onion Dinner Rolls	29
Parmesan-Garlic Biscuits	27

DESSERTS
Angel's Delight	105
BIG Chocolate Cookies	117
Caramel-Marshmallow Delights	123
Chocolate Chip Cookie Dough Pie	113
Cookies & Cream Dessert	109
Easy Butterscotch Bars	101
Lemon Pastries	121
Peanut Butter-Chocolate Bars	103
Pineapple-Cherry Cake	107
Quick Blueberry Crisp	119
Speedy Peanut Butter Cookies	115
Triple Fudge Cake	111

MAINS
BBQ Turkey Meatballs	63
Cheeseburger Bake	67
Cheesy Macaroni & Beef	75
Creamy Chicken Spaghetti	61
Crunchy Corn Chip Chicken	65
Easy Enchilada Casserole	99
Ham & Green Bean Supper	85
Ham & Noodle Skillet	89
Mini Meatloaves	81
No-Fuss Tomato Sauce	95
Noodle Casserole	83
Parmesan Baked Chicken	59
Quick Tuna Casserole	91
Salisbury Steak	69
Saucy Pork Chops	87
Savory Chicken Casserole	55

INDEX

Simple Sloppy Joes	77
Stroganoff Skillet	71
Summertime Salmon Cakes	93
Sweet & Spicy Chicken	53
Swiss Chicken & Stuffing	57
Tex-Mex Chili	73
Wagon Wheel Skillet	79
Zippy Ziti & Broccoli	97

SALADS

5-Cup Ambrosia Salad	25
Best-Ever Broccoli Salad	17
Country Coleslaw	19
Crunchy Corn Chip Salad	13
Redskin Potato Salad	21
Tomato-Feta Salad	15
Waldorf Salad	23

SIDES

15-Minute Parmesan Pasta	49
Baked Zucchini Gratin	45
Cheesy Hashbrowns	47
Cornbread Corn Casserole	37
French-Fried Cauliflower	41
Herbed Corn Bake	43
Scalloped Pineapple	51
Smoky Green Beans	39

How Did Gooseberry Patch Get Started?

Gooseberry Patch started in 1984 one day over the backyard fence in Delaware, Ohio. We were next-door neighbors who shared a love of collecting antiques, gardening and country decorating. Though neither of us had any experience (Jo Ann was a first-grade school teacher and Vickie, a flight attendant & legal secretary), we decided to try our hands at the mail-order business. Since we both had young children, this was perfect for us. We could work from our kitchen tables and keep an eye on the kids too! As our children grew, so did our "little" business. We moved into our own building in the country and filled the shelves to the brim with kitchenware, candles, gourmet goodies, enamelware, bowls and our very own line of cookbooks, calendars and organizers! We're so glad you're a part of our **Gooseberry Patch** family!

For a FREE copy of our **Gooseberry Patch** catalog, write us, call us or visit us online at:

Gooseberry Patch
600 London Rd.
★ P.O. Box 190 ★
Delaware, OH 43015

1·800·854·6673
www.gooseberrypatch.com